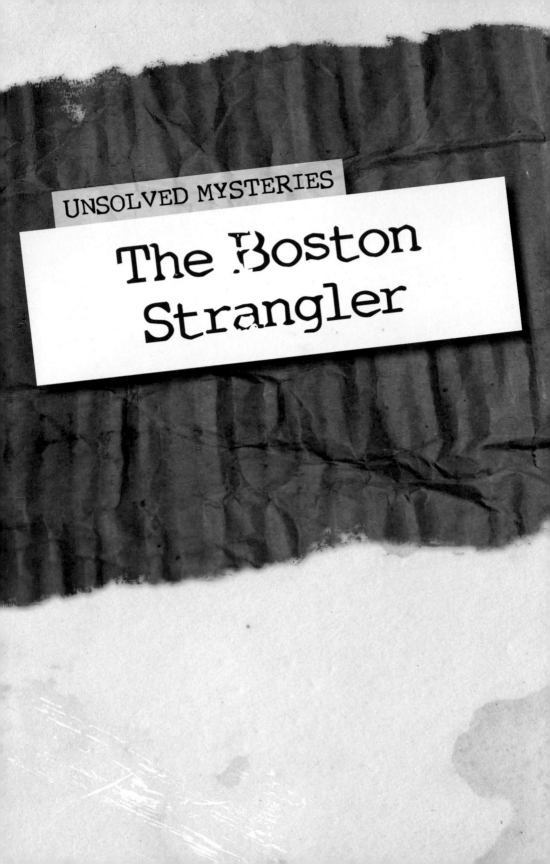

UNSOLVED MYSTERIES

The Boston Strangler

ABDO
Publishing Company

UNSOLVED MYSTERIES

The Boston Strangler

By Paul Hoblin

Content Consultant

Jim Collins
President and Director of Investigations
East Coast Investigative Services Inc.

CREDITS

Published by ABDO Publishing Company, PO Box 398166, Minneapolis, MN 55439. Copyright © 2012 by Abdo Consulting Group, Inc. International copyrights reserved in all countries. No part of this book may be reproduced in any form without written permission from the publisher. The Essential Library™ is a trademark and logo of ABDO Publishing Company.

Printed in the United States of America,
North Mankato, Minnesota
102011
012012

♻ THIS BOOK CONTAINS AT LEAST 10% RECYCLED MATERIALS.

Editor: Melissa York
Copy Editor: Kathryn-Ann Geis
Series design: Becky Daum, Christa Schneider, & Ellen Schofield
Cover production: Christa Schneider
Interior production: Marie Tupy

Library of Congress Cataloging-in-Publication Data
Hoblin, Paul.
 The Boston Strangler / by Paul Hoblin.
     p. cm. -- (Unsolved mysteries)
 Includes bibliographical references.
 ISBN 978-1-61783-299-4
 1. De Salvo, Albert Henry, 1931---Juvenile literature. 2. Serial murderers--Massachusetts--Boston--Case studies--Juvenile literature. 3. Murder--Massachusetts--Boston--Case studies--Juvenile literature. I. Title.
 HV6534.B6H63 2012
 364.152'32092--dc23
                                        2011039552

Table of Contents

Chapter 1

Case Closed?

On January 13, 1967, the *Boston Globe* proclaimed, "DeSalvo is 'Boston Strangler.'"[1] All over Massachusetts, women breathed a sigh of relief. The man feared by many was finally locked up.

Starting in 1962, 11 women living in and around the Boston area had been murdered in similar, brutal ways. Many of these women had been sexually assaulted. One had been stabbed. All had been strangled. The culprit was the Boston Strangler.

The First Victim

On June 14, 1962, Anna Slesers was getting ready to take a bath. She was in her robe, listening to music. Slesers was a 56-year-old Latvian immigrant who had somehow survived the violence in her home country during World War II. That night, she and her son, Juris, were going to attend a memorial service for Latvia's war dead. June 14 is a national day of mourning for Latvians. They never made it.

At approximately 7:00 p.m., Juris knocked on his mother's apartment door. When there was no answer, he thought maybe she had gone to the store. He retreated to the building's front stoop and waited for his mother to return. When she did not come, he returned to her door and knocked a few more times. Still, no one answered.

At approximately 7:45 p.m., he decided to break down the door. Inside, he found his mother's dead body, lying in the hall that led to the bathroom. Her blue robe was torn open. The top of her head was lacerated. One leg was straight; the other was bent

SEEKING PROTECTION: The unsolved murders left many Boston-area women worried for their safety. Many lined up outside of animal shelters, hurrying to adopt stray dogs that could offer some protection from the human predator.

at a 45-degree angle. There was blood in her ear and dripping from her body. She had been sexually assaulted, and she was strangled with the cord of her own robe. The record player was still playing as Juris looked at his mother's murdered body.

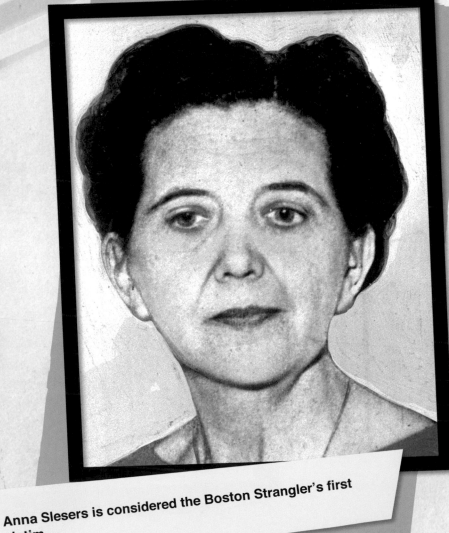

Anna Slesers is considered the Boston Strangler's first victim.

The Second Victim

Just over two weeks later, on June 30, 68-year-old Nina Nichols was on the phone with her sister when her apartment buzzer sounded. As did Slesers, Nichols lived alone.

"Excuse me, Marguerite," she said to her sister over the telephone, "there's my buzzer. I'll call you right back."[2]

But she never called back. That night, she was supposed to drive to Marguerite's house for dinner. She never arrived. After a while, Marguerite became worried enough to tell her husband, who called Nichols's janitor. The janitor reported that Nichols's car was outside, and it appeared she had not left the apartment building. Marguerite's husband had one more request for the janitor: would he be willing to check on Nichols and make sure she was all right?

Nichols did not answer his many knocks, so the janitor unlocked the door with his master key. There, lying on the bedroom rug, was Nichols's dead body. Her legs and eyes were open; so was her pink housecoat. There was blood and mucous on her body. She wore blue tennis shoes. Nichols had been strangled, and two nylons were tied tightly around her neck.

The Murders Continue

Police discovered Helen Blake the same day, June 30. Ida Irga and Jane Sullivan both died later that summer, on August 19 and August 20. Then, thankfully, the violence stopped. For a few months, no new murders were attributed to the Boston Strangler. People hoped the killing spree was over.

However, three months later, Sophie Clark's dead body was discovered on December 5. Clark's murder was followed by Patricia Bissette on December 31, Beverly Samans on May 6, 1963, Evelyn Corbin on September 8, and Joann Graff on November 23. Finally, in what would prove to be the last of the stranglings, 19-year-old Mary Sullivan was found dead in her apartment on January 4, 1964. This last murder was also the most grotesque.

Five of the Boston Strangler's victims, *from left to right*: Patricia Bissette, Ida Irga, Helen Blake, Jane Sullivan, and Sophie Clark

Mary Sullivan is believed to be the final victim of the Boston Strangler.

Mary Sullivan's roommates had just gotten home from a tiring day at work. The bedroom door was open, and though the light was off, Pam could make out Sullivan's body on the bed. Pam assumed her roommate was sleeping, and she headed for the kitchen to help Patricia prepare dinner.

When the food was ready, Pam yelled for Sullivan. After getting no response, she entered the bedroom and flipped the light switch. There was Sullivan—dead. She was propped upright, her back against the headboard, her knees and thighs flexed. Her neck was flexed as well, with a pair of nylons and two scarves tied around it. She had also been sexually assaulted. Next to her foot the killer had left a card: "Happy New Year!" it read.[3]

A Scared City

The public's anxiety mounted with the death count. Door-to-door salesmen could sell nothing. Locksmiths, on the other hand, were suddenly in high demand. So were guard dogs. Police officers and priests had the same advice for women: do not leave your doors unlocked.

Boston Attorney General Edward Brooke eventually seized control of the investigation and created the Boston Strangler Task Force. Brooke appointed Assistant Attorney General John S. Bottomly to lead the investigation. Those on the task force would work exclusively on the Strangler case. Months passed, however, and not a single conviction was made. Whoever was responsible for these grisly murders apparently still roamed the streets, looking for his next victim.

But who was he? According to the media, he was "Mr. S." He was "The Phantom Fiend." He was the Boston Strangler. And, finally, he was Albert DeSalvo. The *Boston Globe* said so, because Albert DeSalvo said so. In 1965, he confessed to killing all

11 victims, plus two more who previously had not been linked with the others.

DeSalvo's confession was detailed and thorough, so the case was closed. Unless, that is, you were a family member of one of the victims or a cop who had been on the case. A large number of them never believed DeSalvo was the killer. Despite his confession, they pointed out, DeSalvo was never convicted of the crime. Besides, they said, his confession may have been detailed, but it was riddled with mistakes.

Decades later, with the help of DNA testing, it appears these doubters might be right. If they are right, a lot of questions remain. Why would an innocent man lie? What did he have to gain? Who is the real Boston Strangler?

Other Victims

Along with the 11 women the media already linked to the Boston Strangler, DeSalvo also took responsibility for the deaths of Mary Brown and Mary Mullen. Brown had been strangled and stabbed to death; but, unlike the other victims, the killer had not tied anything around her neck. Mullen's death was not a homicide at all; she had died of a heart attack. Still, of all the murders DeSalvo took credit for, this one might be the most truthful. He had entered her house intending robbery and was as surprised to see Mullen as she was to see him. Apparently her fright killed her. According to DeSalvo's brother, Richard, DeSalvo wept over the experience and claimed he would never again break into someone's house.

Chapter 2

A Tense Town

DeSalvo didn't confess until 1965. As the murders continued through 1962 and 1963, the public's panic increased. Was there a psycho serial killer on the loose? The media certainly thought so. "Another Silk Stocking Murder," read one headline.[1] "Police Hunt Mad Triple Killer," read another.[2] "Phantom Strangler

Not Just a Strangler

As panic that a mass murderer was on the loose spread, many newspapers were eager to use the public's interest in the event to sell papers. They played up the idea of the murderer as a strangler. One victim, Beverly Samans, had actually been stabbed to death. Nevertheless, the headline in the *Record American* read "Cambridge Girl, 26, Strangled."[3]

Strikes Again,"[4] and "Phantom Strangler Kills Sixth Woman"[5] read two more.

Indeed, the murderer seemed to be a phantom. Women were dying, and yet no screams were heard

Lie Detector

The lie detector test most frequently used is called a polygraph machine. A polygraph tests witnesses' heart rate and blood pressure. The assumption is that when someone is lying, his or her heart rate and blood pressure will increase. This assumption is not always accurate, though, and polygraphs are therefore inadmissible as evidence in most states. They are still used by the police, however, to narrow down a list of suspects.

and no doors were bashed in. Why were these women opening their doors to this man? Why were they not resisting more loudly? And where was the evidence?

By the time the Boston Strangler Task Force was commissioned, this so-called phantom was subject to arguably "the greatest manhunt in the history of modern crime."[6] In addition to the many medical doctors offering their input, specialists in anthropology and forensic law were brought in, as were experts in handwriting. Lie detectors and truth serums were administered. Computer technology, new to the 1960s crime scene, was used to organize all the various sources of information on the killings.

But all of these people and all of these methods were apparently useless—because whoever had

Life in the 1960s

In the 1960s, people were generally less cautious about strangers than they are today. Many people in safe neighborhoods felt comfortable leaving their doors unlocked. Most people were not afraid to open their doors and invite door-to-door salesmen into their homes.

The majority of middle-class, white families had only one source of income. Usually, the men in the family held jobs, while women stayed at home doing household chores or watching children. Many of these women were nervous about being home alone all day with the Strangler on the loose.

committed these ghastly crimes had done so without leaving many clues or having an apparent motive. Why these women? Why now? What did he want? The apartments were often ransacked— drawers were left open, chairs were moved, items and objects were rearranged or tossed on the floor. Was he looking for something? If he was, it did not seem to be money. Again and again, he left without taking any of the victims' most valuable possessions.

With no picture to go on, women all over the Boston area created their own image of the killer. They may never have seen his face, but they could visualize his hands:

NOT ENOUGH TO GO ON: A partial fingerprint was found at the Mary Sullivan crime scene. Unfortunately, police were unable to identify it.

nimble enough to "[scale] the apartment house walls" (evidence at some crime scenes suggested that he had gone through open windows), strong enough to snap necks and destroy other objects (a belt had been ripped in two at Nina Nichols's apartment), and swift enough to render women unconscious before they even had time to scream.[7]

The result of these nicknames, stories, and images was widespread fear. Women refused to open their doors to anyone: salesmen, gas meter readers, telephone installers, political campaigners, even the cops who were trying to find the murderer these women were afraid of.

The Psychology of a Killer

As terrifying as this serial killer was, though, his actions were also strangely reassuring. After all, the cops only had to find one killer, one who apparently killed in a calculated and predictable manner.

Indeed, a pattern had emerged. When 67-year-old Jane Sullivan, the fifth victim, was found dead in her bathtub, the crime scene looked in many ways similar to the previous four. Once again the victim was elderly and white; she was wearing her bathrobe; she lived on her own in an apartment; there was no sign of forced entry. Once again nylons had been knotted around the victim's neck.

The press used this pattern to develop a possible description of the killer. How had he gotten into these women's apartments? Because he "wouldn't impress the average observer as crazy."[8] How had he strangled these women so quickly? Because he "works with his hands, or has a hobby involving handiwork."[9] Why did he choose older women? Because of issues with his mother, who was "a sweet, orderly, neat, compulsive, seductive, punitive, overwhelming woman" (as were, apparently, all the victims).[10] The killer's mother might have liked to "go about half exposed in their apartment but punish him severely for any sexual curiousity [sic]."[11] This would explain why the killer left these women in their ripped-open bathrobes.

In this way, by asking themselves why someone would kill the same way over and over, the police were able to sketch their probable killer. A picture emerged of the Boston Strangler: a man with mother issues who took out his terrifying hatred for her on other women. It all made sense until Sophie Clark was killed.

It was December 5, 1962. At first glance, the crime scene looked almost identical to the others. Like all the victims before her, Clark was wearing an open robe. She had been positioned so she was facing the person who would find her. Her legs were separated. A nylon stocking was knotted around her neck. However, Clark was not elderly. She was 20 years old. And she was not white. She was half white and half African American.

Racial Threats

Sophie Clark's race became an issue when investigators discovered Clark's roommates had been receiving threats for months before her murder. Before moving in with Clark, Audri Adams and Gloria Todd were terrorized in several scary ways. Their cars were vandalized; their safety was threatened over the phone. These incidents appeared to be race related. Todd was African American; Adams was white, but she lived with two women of African-American descent. One day they found the letters *KKK* painted on their front door, which stood for the Ku Klux Klan. The Ku Klux Klan is the name of a hate group that has a history of violence toward African Americans. Due to these facts, some investigators wondered if Clark had been assaulted and killed because of her parentage.

In fact, only one of the last six victims was elderly. If this was the work of the same killer, and the press assumed it was, then the profile of the criminal would need to be discarded, or at least heavily revised. Now it was not just women who looked like the killer's mother who needed to worry. It was all women.

A COPYCAT?: Some people believe the differences between the murders indicates there was more than one murderer. The first five victims, including Slesers and Nichols, were older women. However, the next few victims were younger or younger looking. Was it possible a copycat strangler was also on the loose?

Going Psycho, Going Psychic

The Boston Strangler Task Force had to go back to the drawing board, and it asked for outside help. The governor of Massachusetts offered a $10,000 reward to anyone who could provide information that led to a conviction. The money was meant as an incentive for local detective agencies and regular citizens. An address and a phone number were provided for anyone who could contribute anything relevant to the case.

Thousands of letters and phone calls poured in from all over the world. Sometimes, the writer or caller had good information. Other responses

Police officers went undercover dressed as women, hoping to catch the murderer in the act.

were unhelpful or even crazy. One man offered his theory that a "crew of sex-crazyed Red hitlers" had embedded electronic bugs into the inmates of a prison.[12] According to him, the consequences were catastrophic: robot zombies with homicidal tendencies.

Another informant shared an equally far-fetched but possibly more commonly held theory: the killer had the ability to materialize and dematerialize at will, allowing him to pass through locked doors.

Given some of the other strange advice the task force received from the public, it was not surprising that many concerned citizens suggested hiring a psychic. What is surprising is that John Bottomly, the task force coordinator, took their advice.

The psychic was Peter Hurkos. As a house painter in Holland, he had fallen 35 feet (11 m) and fractured his skull.

Know-It-All?

By all accounts Hurkos knew an extraordinary amount about the various people he encountered during his stay in Boston. While he was looking at the crime scene photos in his hotel room, for instance, a detective entered the room and apologized for being late. His car had broken down, he explained. Hurkos did not believe him. No, Hurkos claimed, he was late because he had decided to hang out with his girlfriend. Apparently, Hurkos was right: the man could only stand and stare at him in amazement.

He was in a coma for three days. When he woke up, his first words were supposedly directed to the doctor: "Don't go! Something terrible will happen!"[13] The doctor, who was planning to go on vacation, dismissed his patient's warning and left the country. A few days later, he was killed.

When Hurkos arrived in Boston, he baffled the investigators and cops in his hotel room. They placed pictures of the crime scenes on his bed, face down, and merely by touching the backs of these pictures, Hurkos was able to describe who the victim on the other side was and what she looked like. He even got down on the floor and mimicked the positions the victims had been left in.

Did he have any idea who the Strangler was? He claimed he did. While touching the nylons of some of the victims, he described the culprit: short, maybe five feet seven inches (1.7 m), 130 to 140 pounds (59 to 64 kg), with a sharp nose and a scar on his left arm. Hurkos added that the murderer never slept on a bed. Hurkos did not know why, but he saw that the man was obsessed with shoes. He could see more, too. The Strangler always washed his hands in the toilet instead of the sink. He was a priest, perhaps, or a doctor. He didn't pay rent and he ate free soup. He had a high voice and a French accent.

Astonishingly, there was a man who fit this description almost perfectly. The height, the weight, the scar, the voice—it all matched Hurkos's description. He even showered with his shoes on.

But Hurkos was wrong. As it turned out, there was no evidence linking this man to any of the murders. How had Hurkos described this man so clearly? How had he done any of the strange feats they had witnessed since his arrival? The answers to these questions were not clear. Ultimately, Hurkos's reported visions were a waste of police time.

What was clear to the public and the media was that Boston's law enforcement was so stumped by the stranglings they had brought in some sort of fortune teller to do their job for them. Many felt law enforcement had managed, through negligence or incompetence, to let a serial murderer go free.

This opinion was unfair, of course; the officers and specialists on the case had done everything they could think of to track down the killer, even exploring the

MENTALLY DISTURBED: The man Hurkos identified as the Strangler was innocent, but he was also mentally disturbed. He had been placed in a mental institution during his interrogation, and afterwards he decided to stay there.

supernatural. They had employed every technological advancement and every expert in the case. Hundreds of suspects had been interrogated.

Unfair or not, one fact could not be denied: 11 women had been murdered in similarly horrific ways, and no one had figured out who committed the murders. Then, in March 1965, Albert DeSalvo confessed to all 11 murders.

Chapter 3

The Measuring Man

Who was Albert DeSalvo? Where had he come from? Why was he voluntarily claiming to be the Boston Strangler? Before hearing DeSalvo's confession, Strangler Task Force Coordinator Bottomly wrote a note to himself: "Start by learning all you can about Albert."[1]

Growing Up

Albert DeSalvo was born on September 3, 1931, just outside Boston. He did not have mother issues, as the psychiatric report suggested the Strangler would, but he definitely had father issues. When DeSalvo was five, his father, Frank, took him to a store and gave him lessons on shoplifting.

Frank also severely abused DeSalvo's mother, Charlotte. Frank witnessed much of this abuse. In many ways, DeSalvo was not just watching; he was learning.

As a 12-year-old, he was arrested for beating up a kid his own age and stealing his money. Five

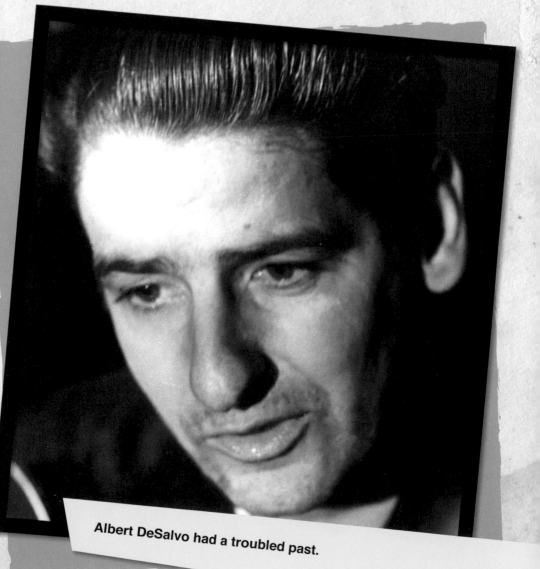

Albert DeSalvo had a troubled past.

weeks later, he and a friend broke into a house and stole $27 worth of jewelry. When he was caught with the stolen goods, he was sent to Lyman School for Delinquent Boys. For the rest of his childhood and adolescence, DeSalvo was sent back and forth between his local school and the reform school. The reason for his returns to Lyman was always theft.

In 1948, DeSalvo enlisted in the army. His unit was sent to Germany, and while there, he met his future wife, Irmgard. When the married couple returned to the United States in 1955, DeSalvo was arrested for molesting a nine-year-old girl. The girl said a soldier showed up at the front door of her house and said he was looking for a place to rent. When she let him in, he fondled her until her brother entered the room. The soldier turned and ran away. Another woman had a similar story. She was able to get a license plate number. The car belonged to Albert DeSalvo. DeSalvo denied responsibility for either incident. Ultimately, both charges were dropped.

Throughout the next several years,

MORE STORIES: According to DeSalvo, his father once sold him and his sisters to a farmer for nine dollars. However, his younger brother Richard says this never happened. "Albert was a great storyteller," he says.[2]

DeSalvo was repeatedly charged with breaking into houses. Though he was found guilty of these crimes, his sentences were suspended again and again. The reasons for these suspensions are today unclear.

DeSalvo was a boxer when he was in the army. He was known as an excellent fighter.

On a two-month family trip to Germany, DeSalvo visited US Army post exchange stores and told the women there that he wrote for the newspaper. The women had been selected, he told them, for a "Best Sweetheart of All" contest. He would then take their measurements and guarantee first prize to the woman who would kiss him. DeSalvo used a similar scam when he got back to the United States.

The Measuring Man

In 1961, a series of distinctive sexual assaults took place in Cambridge, Massachusetts. A man who called himself Johnson showed up on attractive women's doorsteps and told them he was a representative of the Black and White Modeling Agency. The agency, he told these women, was interested in using them for some modeling work and could pay them $40 per hour.

When the women let him inside, he would take their measurements, grope them, then assure them the agency would contact them in the future. Of course, the women never heard from Johnson or his agency again. Enough similar stories were reported to the police that they gave the guy a nickname: the Measuring Man.

Later that year, DeSalvo was caught breaking into a house. A brief chase ensued, ending when a cop fired a warning shot. DeSalvo stopped running and allowed himself to be arrested. He then confessed to being the Measuring Man. Though he was found guilty of the crime, DeSalvo's two-year sentence was reduced to less than a year. In April 1962—two months before the Boston Stranglings began—the Measuring Man was released, free to commit more crimes.

DeSalvo took special satisfaction in having fooled Cambridge women. "I'm not good-looking," he said. "I'm not educated, but I was able to put something over on high-class people."[3]

The Green Man

On the morning of October 27, 1964, another Cambridge woman, Suzanne Macht, woke up and saw a man standing in her bedroom. He was wearing a green work uniform and assured her that she knew him, which was a lie. He stated he was a policeman, then quickly reversed his claim: he was not a cop, he explained, but the cops were chasing him.

When Macht screamed, the man brought out a knife. He promised not to hurt her, then bound her hands together. He gagged and blindfolded her. Pushing up her nightgown, he kissed and fondled her. As he left, he asked her to forgive him.

Macht's story sounded familiar to the cops. Over the last few months, several places had been broken into and several women had been sexually assaulted by a man wearing some sort of work uniform. In every case, both the shirt and the pants were green. Officers gave this man a nickname, too: the Green Man.

Tying Ribbons

DeSalvo and Irmgard had two kids. Their first child, Judy, was born with a rare pelvic disease and had to wear a removable cast. DeSalvo tied ribbons around the cast to keep it secure. Later, some would speculate that the bows he tied on Judy's casts were similar to the ones the Strangler tied around his victims' necks.

Though he had told her not to look at him, Macht was able to give a detailed description of her attacker's face to the department's sketch artist: medium in build, slicked-back black hair, with a prominent nose. A detective looked at the sketch and recognized the man immediately. The Green Man looked exactly like the Measuring Man.

At first, DeSalvo denied any knowledge of the crimes, even though Macht had picked him out of a lineup. After talking with his wife, though, he acknowledged he had committed break-ins and sexual assaults in the area—including some the cops did not know about. As he was driven past Macht's apartment building, he said, "That's where the girl lived who looked at me the other night."[4]

Still, he pled not guilty to all charges. DeSalvo was first charged with the Green Man assaults in late 1964, but the trial did not start until 1967. While awaiting trial, DeSalvo was sent to Bridgewater State Hospital, a psychiatric institution.

DeSalvo was languishing in Bridgewater when he called in attorney F. Lee Bailey, who was representing

GOOD-LOOKING MAN: Many women found DeSalvo attractive. In one headline, the Boston Record American newspaper warned, "Women Beware! He's a Cutie—Keep Chain Lock Bolted."[5]

another inmate at the time. He had something he wanted to confess. DeSalvo admitted that he was not only the Measuring Man and the Green Man . . . he was the Boston Strangler, too. He proceeded to provide convincing details from several of the murders, making his claim seem plausible.

Bridgewater State Hospital in Massachusetts

Chapter 4

Suspect under Scrutiny

When **DeSalvo confessed to being the most notorious serial killer since Jack the Ripper, it seemed to fit.** Here was a man who had a history of breaking into homes. He had developed silent and invisible techniques for picking most kinds of locks.

Here also was a man who had been found guilty of numerous sex crimes. His sexual appetite was apparently insatiable.

SILENT ENTRY: DeSalvo used pieces of plastic from detergent bottles to break into apartments noiselessly.

According to both DeSalvo and his wife, Irmgard, he desired sex constantly. As the Measuring Man, he duped women simply so he could grope them. As the Green Man, he sexually assaulted women at gun- and knifepoint.

UNCONTROLLABLE: In a letter about Irmgard, DeSalvo wrote about his burning love for her. "She told me I would have to learn to control myself," he complained.[1]

One of the baffling oddities about the women the Strangler selected was that they shared no common trait. The Strangler started with older women but then turned to younger ones. He killed mostly white women, but he had also killed an African-American woman. His victims were Protestant, Catholic, and Jewish.

Similarly, DeSalvo's sex drive did not discriminate. His criminal record included sexual assaults on both older and younger women. He had once been arrested for molesting a nine-year-old girl.

Of course, though there seemed to be no pattern to the choice of victims, there was certainly a progression to the gruesomeness of their deaths. Each murder was more horrifying than the one before it.

The media claimed DeSalvo's criminal history followed a similar progression. The Measuring

Man had fondled his victims. The Green Man had threatened, bound, and sexually assaulted them. The media speculated the Boston stranglings were the next terrifying step in this progression of violence.

Bailey, who had heard DeSalvo confess, agreed. So did Bottomly. Most important, so did DeSalvo himself. Over the next several months, DeSalvo not only took credit for the crimes, he described each and every murder in alarmingly specific detail.

Becoming More Violent?

This perceived progression of increasing violence did not actually happen. The Green Man assaults took place after the Boston stranglings. For DeSalvo to have been both the Boston Strangler and the Green Man, he would have had to become less violent, not more. But because of the order in which the evidence of the case unfolded, it was easy to imagine evil evolving rather than decreasing.

While recounting Beverly Samans's murder, DeSalvo described the woman as built like an opera singer, exactly what she was training to become. He said she was hard of hearing, which was also true. Samans was a student, he said—and, again, he was right.

Then he discussed the layout and look of her apartment. He correctly mentioned the piano and typewriter and where they were located. He said the shades were pulled down, and indeed they were left closed. His description of where and how the murderer left Samans's dead body was confirmed by the police reports: face-up on a couch with a rag stuffed in her mouth.

F. Lee Bailey believed DeSalvo's confession.

Polygraph Test

Bailey wanted to have DeSalvo as a client. He thought DeSalvo should take a polygraph test to determine whether he was telling the truth about being the Strangler. Bottomly agreed with Bailey. Bailey showed up with the lie detecting equipment, but he was turned away at the door because he was not DeSalvo's official lawyer. DeSalvo already had a lawyer, Jon Asgeirsson, and Bailey therefore had no right to interact with another attorney's client. Soon, Bailey did officially become one of DeSalvo's attorneys—but for an unknown reason the polygraph test was never given.

He knew similar details about all the victims and all the stranglings. The details were so specific, some became convinced the only person who could know all these details was indeed the Boston Strangler.

There were officers who were certain DeSalvo was the Strangler. Detectives John Donovan and Edward Sherry were two of them. Captain James McDonald thought that if DeSalvo was not the killer, he "must have been looking over the Strangler's shoulder."[2]

Others, though, were less sure. "There isn't a cop in Cambridge who ever believed DeSalvo was the Strangler," said Captain William R. Burke Jr.[3] Several other officers echoed his statement. And they were not alone. Several of the victims' relatives never believed DeSalvo's confession, either. Diane Sullivan

Dodd, sibling of the last victim, said, "I just knew in my heart that this creep didn't kill my sister."[4]

Many members of the police force did not believe DeSalvo committed the Boston Strangler murders.

Chapter 5

No Positive IDs

Given all the evidence against him, how could anyone doubt that DeSalvo was the Strangler? On the surface, he fit the profile perfectly. However, for a sexual predator, DeSalvo was not a violent man. In fact, most people who knew DeSalvo describe him as harmless—including, astonishingly enough, one of his victims. "I did not think he had the brutality to strangle women," one detective said.[1] "He was a very gentle guy," another cop added.[2]

RUNAWAY: One ex-Cambridge detective says that DeSalvo "didn't fight back" when women resisted him; instead, "[he] took off."[3]

Their point is not that he was guiltless of all crimes; DeSalvo had performed many unlawful and despicable acts. But was he a serial killer? Most people who knew him do

A Gentle Guy

One of DeSalvo's many victims described him to authorities as "a gentle guy."[4] Her description of DeSalvo was not accurate, of course—what he had done to her and other women was far from gentle behavior—but she was not alone in thinking DeSalvo treated his victims with far less brutality than the Boston Strangler treated his victims.

not think so. Of course, their opinions would likely change if there were any evidence linking DeSalvo to any of the crime scenes. But no such evidence exists.

Missing Evidence

When the Strangler was in the midst of carrying out his vicious crimes, it seemed as though he showed up and vanished without a trace. But this was not actually true. The killer left physical evidence and eyewitness accounts. And none of this evidence led back to DeSalvo.

On the day Joann Graff was murdered, for instance, a man knocked on one of her neighbor's doors. He asked to see a Joann, but mispronounced her name: *Joan* instead of *Jo-ann*. The neighbor explained the man had the wrong apartment and then pointed him to the right one. After Graff's dead body was found, this man became a prime suspect. It was not DeSalvo. The neighbor was shown a picture of DeSalvo and could not identify him.

On the same day, a man visited a local bar twice—first at approximately 2:00 p.m., before Graff's murder, and then again at approximately 4:30 p.m., after the murder. The owner of the bar had never seen the man before. On his second visit, this man looked agitated and unkempt. His clothes were wrinkled.

The description of these clothes matched the one given by Joann Graff's neighbor. Was this the same man who had asked for Joan instead of Joann? The owner of the bar also could not identify a picture of DeSalvo.

A MEMORABLE DRINK: The owner of the bar remembered the man because he asked for a Lucky Beer, a brand that was not sold in Boston.

Differing Physical Descriptions

A woman who lived in an apartment building next to Mary Sullivan spotted a man standing in Sullivan's building on the day she was killed. He was tall, she said, with reddish-brown hair. She was given a picture of DeSalvo. She did not think it was the man she had seen.

Some recently smoked Salem-brand cigarette butts were in an ashtray in Sullivan's apartment. Neither Sullivan nor her roommates smoked Salems. DeSalvo did not smoke at all.

At 2:30 p.m. on December 5, 1962, the day Sophie Clark was murdered, a woman talked with a man who claimed he was there to paint her home. His name was Thompson, he said. Then he started talking about her body, asking if she had ever considered modeling.

The woman got rid of the man by claiming her husband was sleeping in the next room. After DeSalvo claimed to have murdered Clark,

Follow the Evidence

Along with eyewitnesses' inability to identify DeSalvo, there were pieces of physical evidence that pointed to a different killer. Though DeSalvo did not smoke, a Salem cigarette butt was found in the toilet of Clark's apartment. She and her roommates smoked, but that did not explain how the Salem cigarette had gotten into the toilet. In Beverly Samans' apartment, investigators found a handprint on a television screen—probably a man's. Though the handprint was never identified, it was conclusively determined that it did not belong to DeSalvo.

one had to wonder: had he visited this other woman before killing Clark? Had he used his old Measuring Man model agency trick? Was this proof that DeSalvo had been in the area and on the hunt?

The answer to all these questions appears to be no. The man this woman encountered had combed-back, honey-colored hair. He was either a dark-skinned white man or a light-skinned African-American man.

Later that same day, another resident of the area described a man with almost identical physical details. The man he saw was African American with light skin. He had his long hair combed back and wore a dark jacket, as had the man claiming to be Thompson.

Even later that day—after Clark had been murdered—another woman had a bizarre conversation with a man at her door. Sweat poured from him as he asked to borrow a book. He had sandy hair, light brown skin, and a dark jacket.

These three descriptions formed a picture of a fairly specific man—a man who looked nothing like DeSalvo. Nonetheless, the woman who first described the man called Thompson was brought in to see DeSalvo, just in case she could identify him in person. She could not.

DeSalvo had pale skin with dark brown hair and brown eyes.

Composite Sketches

Drawings made by sketch artists are often important first clues to finding a criminal. These artists need to be good at more than drawing—they also need to be good at helping witnesses remember specific physical details about a suspect. One way they do this is to show witnesses several pictures of different facial features, including noses, mouths, and eyes; the artist takes whatever features the witness chooses and combines them to make a composite picture.

Sheridan Falls Police Department
1800 Witherson Ave
Sheridan Falls, NY
To be distributed to all deputies and superintendents
of Farrel County

October 23
Case no. 4555300-01

WANTED

FOR HOMICIDE / ARMED ROBBERY

Suspect Description:
Sex: Male
Age: 31
Height: 5'10"
Weight: 180
Hair Color: Dark brown
Eye Color: Unknown

Wanted for homicide and armed robbery of Kosak Convenience Store on the corner of 34 and Higgins on the night of Sept. 24th. Suspect was last seen with a dark navy winter hat, blue jeans, and black sweatshirt.
If you have any information regarding this incident, call the Sheridan Falls Police Dept. Callers will remain anonymous.

W-203-01

Nor could the woman who came with her, a woman whom many believed was the only survivor of a Boston Strangler attack. Her name was Erika Wilsing, and she had been assaulted on February 18, 1963. The man had promised not to hurt her if she did not struggle. However, she fought back ferociously. When the man put his hand around her neck, she bit into it until he let go and ran away.

A handyman working in the area that day said he watched a man go into Wilsing's apartment building.

A few minutes later, he heard a scream. Shortly after that, he saw the same man exit the building in a blue raincoat.

The handyman was given a picture of DeSalvo, and—as had everyone else who witnessed or heard something suspicious—he did not recognize the man who wanted credit for the Boston stranglings. If DeSalvo was the Boston Strangler, why had no one seen him near the crime scenes before or after the crimes were committed?

Chapter 6

DeSalvo's Confession

During the months of August and September 1965, while he was being held at Bridgewater, DeSalvo described the various ways he had killed all 11 victims. Bottomly interrogated DeSalvo and recorded his confession. But there were holes in these confessions.

For one thing, DeSalvo was unable to describe the murders in their proper order—even though, by all accounts, he had a photographic memory. More alarmingly, the surviving transcripts of his confession are riddled with DeSalvo's questionable, skewed, or outright wrong answers to Bottomly's questions.

Even when DeSalvo eventually came up with the right answer, he would often begin with the wrong answer. When DeSalvo described Anna Slesers's blue robe, he said, "It was just dark." However, he contradicted himself in the very next sentence: "It was a navy, a light navy blue you might call it—light."[1]

Why had DeSalvo changed his answer? Had Bottomly looked at him a certain way to indicate he was mistaken? There was no camera in the room, so it is impossible to know the answers to these questions. One could argue that this sort of inaccuracy is minor.

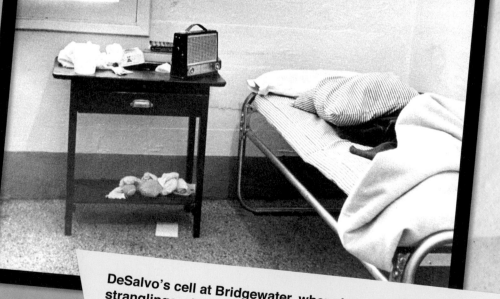

DeSalvo's cell at Bridgewater, where he confessed to the stranglings while awaiting trial for the Green Man crimes

However, the transcripts demonstrate DeSalvo's difficulty with major details, too.

When police found Ida Irga's body, her feet had been propped up on two chairs. These chairs stood upright, but DeSalvo described laying the chairs on their backs. When police found Beverly Samans's body, they counted 17 stab wounds. DeSalvo claimed to have stabbed her three to five times. Later, he raised the number to seven. He also had difficulty with the murder weapon. DeSalvo said he used a switchblade and then threw it into a swamp, but evidence proved the killer actually used one of Samans's own knives.

Memory Test

Forensic psychologist Dr. Ames Robey tested DeSalvo's memory. During a staff meeting with approximately eight people, Robey had DeSalvo walk in, glance at those in the room, and walk out. At the next day's staff meeting, Robey made sure all the staff members were dressed differently and sitting in different spots. Once again he brought DeSalvo into the room and asked his patient to describe what the people in the room had looked like the day before. DeSalvo passed Robey's test with ease.

Some of his most perplexing mistakes occurred when discussing Mary Sullivan's murder with another attorney, Jon Asgeirsson. First, DeSalvo said, he gagged Sullivan; then he yanked her sweater over her head and sexually assaulted her. He claimed to have left a knife next to her bed. This description was certainly graphic, but it was also completely wrong. The killer had done none of these things.

Missing Details

Even with Bottomly's help, DeSalvo also failed to get many details of Clark's murder right. For example, DeSalvo claimed Clark had her glasses off when she opened the apartment door—but according to her roommates, this was highly unlikely. Clark's eyesight was terrible, and she rarely took off her glasses. DeSalvo also got the color of her bathrobe wrong. He said it was white when it was actually a blue floral print. DeSalvo told Bottomly that Clark was wearing black high heels, when in fact she had been wearing brown loafers. He also stated there were glass bottles and musical instruments in her apartment; there were none of these items.

What DeSalvo omitted from the depiction was equally perplexing. DeSalvo, who was usually more than willing to share the gory details of the crime, even ones that never happened, left out the graphic details of her sexual assault. Later, when confessing his crimes to Bottomly, he did mention the missing details—but why then and not earlier?

Indeed, his revised version of events seems to point to another possibility: Bottomly, it appears, helped DeSalvo get his story right. In some instances, Bottomly even showed DeSalvo close-up photographs of a crime scene prior to taking his confession.

Again and again, Bottomly helped DeSalvo come up with the right answers to his questions. He showed DeSalvo pictures of the crime scenes. He asked leading questions. Sometimes he supplied DeSalvo with the correct information, as in this excerpt from the Clark confession:

```
DESALVO: I stripped her naked. I stripped her naked,
I do recall this.

BOTTOMLY: Was she wearing a bra?

DESALVO: Yes.

BOTTOMLY: Was she wearing anything else also?

DESALVO: There could have been a half-slip.

BOTTOMLY: Anything else?

DESALVO: A white . . . she had stockings on and
shoes.

BOTTOMLY: Now, did you do anything else with the
bra?

DESALVO: The bra I could have put around her neck,
but I'm not sure on this one.

BOTTOMLY: Did you put anything else around her neck?
Other than the bra and her stocking?

DESALVO: Yes . . . a kerchief . . . no, let me
think. Let me think . . .

BOTTOMLY: Something she might be wearing?
```

```
DESALVO: Yes.

BOTTOMLY: What?

DESALVO: [A] blouse. Ah, this is a [snaps fingers]
. . . let me think . . .[2]
```

Bottomly was leading the suspect, something an interrogator is never supposed to do. As soon as DeSalvo claimed he stripped off Clark's clothes, Bottomly helped him re-dress her. Whenever DeSalvo got stuck or stopped talking, Bottomly prodded his confession forward.

When confessing to Jane Sullivan's murder, DeSalvo realized he was not actually sure whether he took off her bra—so he asked Bottomly: "It went off, right?"[3] Bottomly told him that it had.

Untrustworthy Confession

Bottomly was aware DeSalvo's confession was not airtight. He said as much to DeSalvo: a grand jury, Bottomly explained, was unlikely to find DeSalvo's words persuasive. By September 29, 1965—the last day of DeSalvo's confession—it must have been clear to Bottomly that the tapes, all 54 hours of them, would be of little use to prosecutors or the Boston Strangler Task Force.

Then, suddenly, Bottomly resigned from his job. The reason for his resignation is controversial, but many feel it had to do with the confession tapes and his questionable performance as the interrogator. Attorney General Edward Brooke said Bottomly quit after a fight with someone in the office that had nothing to do with the Strangler case. Whatever the reason, Bottomly took the confession tapes with him when he left.

However, DeSalvo was clearly guilty of his Green Man crimes—the victims would testify to that—so no matter what happened with the Strangler confession, he was going to be locked up for a long time.

Surprising Details

DeSalvo's confession may have been loaded with errors, but it was also loaded with details. Often, these details were dead-on. But, if he was not the killer, how could he know so much about the killings?

Part of the answer might have to do with DeSalvo's memory. According to Dr. Ames Robey, the forensic psychologist who helped the Strangler Bureau assess suspects, DeSalvo had "absolute, complete, one hundred per cent total photographic recall."[4] Others were impressed by DeSalvo's memory. Two of DeSalvo's lawyers, Jon Asgeirsson and Tom Troy, have talked about their client's incredible ability to recall information.

Of course, a photographic memory would not help DeSalvo unless he had access to information about the murders. Unless he were in the victims' apartments at the time they were strangled, how could DeSalvo possibly know so much about the crimes?

Newspaper Accounts

The first and most obvious answer is that he could have read the paper. Reports of the stranglings were both precise and graphic. The most detailed accounts of the murders were often printed in the *Record American*.

DeSalvo knew incredibly detailed information about Beverly Samans. He talked about her aspirations to be an opera singer and mentioned she was hard of hearing. He knew that she had a typewriter and a piano in her apartment and that she was found face-up, on a couch, with a rag in her mouth. However, all of this information and more was detailed in the newspapers.

When describing the scene of Helen Blake's murder, the *Record American* notes that some of the drawers were

Silent Visitor

According to his family members, DeSalvo was fascinated with the Boston Strangler crimes. He may have visited the crime scenes just to see the apartments. He even admitted to doing this during a conversation with Dr. Robey. The claim could be possible, considering his history of breaking into apartments all over the Boston area.

pulled out of a desk and a bureau, a large black trunk was moved from the bedroom closet and placed on a chair, the lock on the trunk had been jimmied open with a knife, and the tip of the knife had broken off and remained inside the lock.

The account keeps going, locating key objects and speculating how they got there and how they were used. The next day the *Record American* provided more: her coffee cup, unused, had been set on the living room table; a footlocker with towels in it had been opened, apparently by the killer.

Repeatedly, and with increasing detail, the Boston papers described each crime scene and each crime. On January 23, the *Record* put all this information into a chart. This worksheet listed the victims' names, ages, and times of death. It also included when their bodies were found, what clothing they were wearing, and whether the killer had raided their apartments. Even the victims' jobs and hobbies were listed.

Law Enforcement Leaks

Strangler Task Force members acknowledged that supposedly confidential information was repeatedly given to the media. A medical examiner held press conferences and talked openly about the bodies he examined. Author Gerold Frank was given full access to the files even though the cases were ongoing.

Office boys made copies of all the case files. Due to lack of space, these copies were spread out on desks and left in the open. The files were available to so many people that it became impossible to know who read what and who said what to the media or the general public.

To this day, the taped confession has never been made public in its entirety. Those who have heard it, including author Susan Kelly, claim that it proves DeSalvo's innocence. If they are right, and DeSalvo is not the Boston Strangler, who is?

The Boston stranglings took place in neighborhoods similar to this one.

Chapter 7

The Real Boston Strangler

DeSalvo had at least one other source of information: his fellow inmates at Bridgewater State Hospital, where he awaited his trial for the Green Man crimes. There was a good reason at least one of them might have had accurate information. A handful of them were suspected of being the Boston Strangler themselves.

George Nassar

On September 29, 1964, a woman and her 14-year-old daughter turned into a gas station. As they pulled up to the gas pumps they saw one man on his knees and another man standing over him.

The man on his knees was likely pleading for his life; the man standing over him had a gun, and he fired it. The woman and her daughter watched

This corridor at Bridgewater held DeSalvo's cell. At Bridgewater, DeSalvo met several inmates who were potential suspects.

helplessly as the man toppled from his knees. He was then shot several more times.

They watched, frozen in fear, as the man with the gun began walking toward their car. When he reached the driver's side, he pounded on the door. Then he raised the gun and pointed it at them. The trigger clicked twice, but the gun was empty.

At approximately the same time, two men in a truck pulled into the gas station. They watched the man run from the woman's car and get into a car of his own. The man was slim, tan, and had dark hair.

The daughter and mother were shown dozens of mug shots of potential suspects. No, they agreed, none of them looked like the man at the gas station. But they were certain that, if shown the right man, they would know it. They provided a thorough description of the man to a sketch artist. Based on the drawing, they were shown another picture, and they identified the man as the killer. The picture showed Nassar. He was brought to the station and put in a lineup. Once again, the women were able to pick him out.

Nassar was suspected of having mental issues and was sent to Bridgewater for observation, where he met DeSalvo. When Erika Wilsing, believed to be the only survivor of a Strangler attack, was brought to Bridgewater, she did not recognize DeSalvo. But she did recognize Nassar. Marcella Lulka, one of the key possible witnesses in the Clark murder, visited Bridgewater that day as well.

Police often show witnesses a lineup of potential suspects to help them identify criminals.

Viewing the Suspect

In order to get a good look at DeSalvo, Marcella Lulka and Erika Wilsing pretended to be relatives waiting to see other inmates. They sat in the visitors' waiting room and watched DeSalvo talk to someone else. Once DeSalvo left, the two women said they did not recognize him. However, they did recognize Nassar, who happened to be there to talk to his social worker.

She said DeSalvo did not look like the man who had rung her doorbell the day Clark was killed. But, except for his hair color, Nassar was the spitting image of him.

Peter Burton

A brilliant former Harvard student, Peter Burton withdrew from the school after being arrested for the possession of explosives. He had built a bomb and planned to detonate it along a highway. A mechanical failure was the only thing that prevented the explosion.

On January 22, 1964, Burton was arrested again, this time for pulling a woman toward his car. The woman turned out to be his wife. When asked why he was pulling her, he said he wanted to take her on a picnic. The cop pointed out that it was the middle of winter. "It's never too cold to have fun," Burton replied.[1] At the time he was dressed as Othello, a character from Shakespeare who kills his wife out of jealousy.

Burton talked openly about his ferocious hatred toward women. He planned to invent something that made a huge profit. With the money, he would purchase an island next to Australia and put up a fence around it. No women allowed.

In particular, he hated nurses. Both his mother and his wife were nurses, and both left him feeling enraged and inadequate. After being refused sex by his wife, he said, he would wander the streets looking for a woman to, in his words, destroy. All of the first five strangling victims had close connections with the medical field.

When Burton was sent to Bridgewater, Dr. Robey learned that Burton had been in the area on the days Anna Slesers, Nina Nichols, Helen Blake, Ida Irga, and Jane Sullivan were killed. Burton was at Bridgewater with DeSalvo.

Related Murders?

A few years later, several more women were viciously killed in Michigan. The murders were similar enough to the stranglings in Boston that Dr. Robey looked up Peter Burton. Sure enough, he was a student at the University of Michigan at the time. He was also known to be living in Los Angeles, California, when a series of murders called the Hillside stranglings occurred. Robey wondered whether Burton was involved, but authorities thought not. Someone else was convicted for one of the Michigan murders, and two others were found guilty of the stranglings in California.

Arthur Barrows

Arthur Barrows was yet another Strangler suspect
staying at Bridgewater at the same time as DeSalvo.
Unlike Burton, Barrows was not intelligent. But
similar to Burton, he had a deep hatred of women.
Barrows was a towering, filthy man. Despite this,
he had the ability to appear, hide, and reappear
seemingly at will.

He tried to kill his own mother by throwing
her down the stairs. She survived, but not for long.
At the hospital, she died of a heart attack. She was
discovered lying on the floor, even though sides had
been put up on her bed to keep her from falling.
Some thought that Barrows had tossed her to the
ground before leaving the hospital. The intravenous
tubes had been ripped out of her body.

On the morning of April 9, 1963, a young
woman was on her way home from church and
decided to save time by going down an alley. Out
of nowhere, a tall, terrifying man emerged and
began to choke her with her scarf. Before her throat
constricted she was able to let out a kick and,
somehow, a scream. A college student passing by
heard her and came running. When he found her,
she was unconscious. The attacker had run from the
scene.

Close by, another woman was attacked that day. The man blamed her for his problems, then tried to throttle her. She fought and kicked until he fled. The attacks took place only a few blocks from Anna Slesers's apartment. Each of these women identified Barrows as their strangler.

But was he *the* Strangler? According to his sister, Barrows confessed to the crimes repeatedly. And the calendar supported his confession. During 1962, Barrows had been a patient at Boston State Hospital. According to their records, he was missing from the hospital on June 14, June 30, July 11, August 19, and August 21, the dates on which the first five stranglings occurred. Barrows was committed to Bridgewater but not charged with the stranglings.

OUT OF PRISON: In 1961, Barrows had been paroled after spending 16 years in prison for murdering a shopkeeper.

Chapter 8

More Suspects

Along with DeSalvo's fellow inmates at Bridgewater, other men were considered prime suspects in at least one of the murder cases. One suspect was Bradley Schereschewsky. Schereschewsky fit the assumed profile of the Strangler better than DeSalvo. In 1959, at the age of 24, Schereschewsky was incarcerated at Danvers State Hospital. He was charged with sexually assaulting his own mother. When his father tried to intervene on his wife's behalf, Bradley beat him up brutally.

His violent sexual behavior toward his mother gave him a motive for murdering the first five women, all of whom were elderly. Was

Schereschewsky doing to these women what he had wanted to do to his mother? It seemed possible.

Just as alarmingly, each of the murders of the elderly victims took place while Schereschewsky was on extended release from various medical institutions. There was also evidence placing him in close proximity to several of the stranglings.

Robert Cambell

When DeSalvo confessed to killing Evelyn Corbin, he said he used her front door. Some consider this more proof that DeSalvo was lying about being the Strangler. The killer, it appeared, had not used the front door. He had used the fire escape. He left a doughnut there to prove it. Corbin did not eat doughnuts.

Corbin's killer likely came in through a fire escape.

On Saturday,
September 7, the
night before Corbin's
death, a man named
Robert Cambell
purchased a box of
doughnuts. When
Sunday morning
arrived, he pocketed
some of the doughnuts and disappeared for several
hours. When he returned, Cambell and the teenage
girl he was living with drove to New York. He told
her to turn off the radio because he did not want to
hear any news reports.

A PROWLER: Corbin had called the police several times in the days leading up to her death. Each time she claimed there was a prowler outside her building.

Cambell's wife had recently thrown him out
of the house. Soon after leaving town, Cambell's
girlfriend left him, presumably fearing for her own
safety. Cambell later served prison time for other
sexual assaults.

Daniel Pennacchio

Beverly Samans, considered by the media to be the
eighth woman killed by the Strangler, worked at the
Walter E. Fernald State School, a school for children
with developmental disabilities, from 1959 to 1962.
A suspect named Daniel Pennacchio was a student at
Fernald until 1963.

No Warrant

Despite all the accuracies in Pennacchio's confession, there must have been some inaccuracies as well, at least enough for the judge to refuse the prosecution's request for a warrant. A warrant gives police permission to search a suspect's property for clues in a case.

Upon entering the real world, Pennacchio's behavior became increasingly creepy. He would stand next to his car and leer at women as they walked by. Sometimes he would invite these women to get in his car, an offer they quickly refused. He was finally taken into custody when a nurse saw him on hands and knees peering under the door of the women's bathroom at a local hospital.

At the station, Pennacchio announced he had killed Samans. His confession was in many cases more accurate than DeSalvo's. While DeSalvo said he stabbed Samans no more than seven times, Pennacchio claimed to have stabbed her approximately 15 times. She was actually stabbed 17 times.

According to Pennacchio, he had arrived at Samans's place just before midnight on May 5. Indeed, Samans had been home at that time.

While he was there, Pennacchio said, he had talked with her about her graduate school thesis paper. Sure enough, when the cops arrived at the crime scene, a page from her thesis was in the carriage of her typewriter.

Several other details in Pennacchio's confession were correct. The murderer had gagged the victim with a rag, he had put a cloth over her head, and he had used a knife from her kitchen. Despite the accuracy of his confession, many people, including the judge at his hearing, believed the man was delusional. The search warrant detectives sought was denied, and Pennacchio was released from prison.

Any ongoing investigation into Pennacchio's guilt ended when he drowned while swimming with

Pennacchio knew several specific details about Samans's life, including information about her graduate thesis.

two teenage girls a few weeks later. Pennacchio dove into the water from a bridge. The water was shallow, and he hit the bottom headfirst.

Jules Rothman

On the morning of Monday, December 31, 1962, Jules Rothman visited Patricia Bissette's apartment. Bissette was Rothman's secretary, and he was going to give her a ride to work. But Bissette was not home, or if she was there, she did not answer the door.

At his office soon after, Rothman tried calling Bissette, but she still did not answer. An hour passed. After repeatedly asking a woman in the office what he should do, Rothman finally decided to return to the apartment. The janitor did not have a key to Bissette's place so the two men decided to climb through the window. Rothman went first. After accidentally knocking over a Christmas tree, he searched the apartment. When he got to the bedroom he saw that Bissette was home—and dead.

It did not take long for the police to figure out two things: Rothman, a married man with children, was Bissette's lover, and Bissette was pregnant. Both of these pieces of information were revealed by physical evidence. A card was found in her apartment that read "To Patsy . . . Love Jules."[1] An autopsy showed Bissette was carrying a child.

Rothman confirmed he knew about the baby, but said he was not sure if it was his. He also said he had met with a friend the previous Friday to discuss Bissette's situation.

The detective's next question was point-blank. Was Rothman looking for a doctor who would perform an abortion? Abortion

Crime Scene Description

Rothman said a lot of things that seemed a little off to the authorities. One of them occurred at the scene of the crime. Upon finding Bissette's body, he described her in grotesque terms. Her eyes were bulging, he said; her tongue was swollen. He also mentioned the stocking tied around her neck. When the police arrived, however, they saw that her eyes were not bulging and her tongue was not swollen. Because the murderer had tucked her in up to her chin, they had to remove the blanket to see the stocking that had been used to strangle her. How had Rothman known about the stocking if it was not visible?

was illegal in the United States in 1962. Rothman's answer was less direct: not exactly, he said. He was looking for general solutions to the problem. And he had found one: the friend told him about a convent in Buffalo, New York, where Bissette could live until the baby was born. Later that night, Rothman claimed, he had visited Bissette at her apartment, and she had agreed to go to Buffalo.

The friend did not remember their conversation quite the same way, though. The friend said Rothman was looking for an abortionist. Thus, Rothman had a motive: his lover was pregnant, potentially with his baby, and he might have wanted to get rid of both of them.

In fact, the more investigators looked, the more motives they uncovered. Rothman, it turned out, was having large financial difficulties, and Bissette had recently become a major stockholder in the company. Had Rothman killed Bissette for her stock in the company?

Both of these motives still needed to be clarified. What was clear was that Rothman had a shaky alibi for his whereabouts on the Sunday Bissette was murdered. He was asked to take a lie detector test, and he failed.

Lie Detector

The official report after Rothman took the lie detector test said, "Reactions exhibited on this chart indicate that he is not telling the truth."[2] Unfortunately, exactly what Rothman was lying about was never determined. Due to his history with the victim, his questionable alibi, and his poor performance on the lie-detector test, Rothman was for a brief time considered the primary suspect in Bissette's murder. Investigators strongly considered bringing the evidence against Rothman to the grand jury—but then DeSalvo confessed to the crime, and the case against Rothman was never pursued.

So Who Is the Boston Strangler?

Was the Boston Strangler Nassar? Burton? Barrows? Schereschewsky? Cambell? Pennacchio? Rothman?

All of these men were at one time prime suspects in the case, and for good reason. Several of them fit the profile investigators had developed early on in their search for the Strangler. Others could be placed at or near some of the crime scenes. Still others confessed to the murders.

A case can be made that each one of these men was a more persuasive suspect than DeSalvo. So why, when DeSalvo started confessing, did everyone believe him?

Many of these men seemed to have specific motives for selecting victims, but DeSalvo did not; he said he picked the women at random.

Chapter 9

A Madman's Motives

Of course, most people didn't believe DeSalvo's confession—at least, not those who knew him or the case well. Irmgard, DeSalvo's wife, asked him, "Why are you telling everyone you're the Boston Strangler? This is crazy!"[1]

What would possess a man to take credit for so many brutal murders? As it turned out, there were several reasons. DeSalvo may not have been able to provide a motive for killing the Strangler victims, but he had at least three good motives for confessing to the crimes.

Fame

Everyone who knew DeSalvo will tell you he loved to brag. Often, this bragging turned to stretching the truth, which turned to outright lying. "He had a deep-rooted need to be famous," says a former Cambridge detective.[2] "If you said to him, 'Hey, I did twenty burglaries,' he'd say, 'That's nothing, I did two hundred,'" explains a former orderly at Bridgewater.[3]

FLED THE SCENE: Soon after DeSalvo's confession, Irmgard DeSalvo fled to Colorado with her children to avoid the publicity.

DeSalvo in prison, 1973. He was well known among inmates for his love of bragging.

When Dr. Robey asked DeSalvo how many women he had assaulted, he said 600. Then he changed his mind. A thousand. Clearly, the man wanted people to be impressed by him. If he could not be famous, he could at least be infamous. DeSalvo wanted to be the Strangler so badly, Robey thought he may have briefly begun to believe he really was the Strangler.

Strangler Chokers

In prison, DeSalvo tried other ways to make money on his reputation as the Strangler. He wrote and recorded a song entitled "Strangler in the Night." He also tried selling necklaces, which he called Strangler chokers.

Fortune

Along with his good friend and fellow Strangler suspect Nassar, DeSalvo hatched several plans to make money. At the time, there was a $10,000 reward being offered to anyone who could supply information that led to the Strangler's capture. Nassar and DeSalvo thought, incorrectly, that $10,000 would be given for each victim—a total of $110,000 altogether.

The deal they made was simple: Nassar would tell his attorney that he had information about the Strangler, and DeSalvo would confess to each of the crimes. Then they would split the money right down the middle.

Besides the reward money, DeSalvo believed people would pay good money for his story. Magazines would pay him huge sums of money, as would book publishers. If they made a movie about him, he and his family would be set for life.

Fate

Bailey, Nassar's attorney as well as DeSalvo's, assured DeSalvo he would likely never be a free man again. Whether or not he was the Boston Strangler, he was most definitely the Green Man, and the crimes he had committed under that name were bad enough to send him to jail for a very long time.

The only question was: Where would DeSalvo be locked up? In a prison, or in a hospital? By claiming he was the Boston Strangler, DeSalvo hoped he would be placed in a top-notch mental institution with doctors who wanted to study the brain of a serial killer. That sounded a lot better to DeSalvo than rotting away in jail.

Selling the Strangler

Those who knew DeSalvo may not have believed his confession, but the media bought it completely. The *Record American* announced that the Boston Strangler—not a suspect in the strangling crimes but the actual Strangler—was being kept in Bridgewater. A television crew showed up almost instantly. By the time DeSalvo's trial started, Gerold Frank's book *The Boston Strangler* had become a bestseller.

DeSalvo and *Strangler* had become synonymous. Of course, DeSalvo was not on trial for any stranglings—there was no physical evidence linking him to any of those murders. Instead, he was on trial for being the Green Man.

But few people seemed to realize this. Bailey acknowledged openly that DeSalvo was the Strangler. Yes, he admitted, his client had committed several sexual assaults, but he had also horrifically murdered many women in 18 months.

MISLEADING HEADLINE: "Jury Holds Strangler's Fate," said the *Record American*, even though the trial had nothing to do with any of the stranglings.[4]

Surely, Bailey argued, this man cannot be considered sane. Surely, Bailey continued, he should be sent to a medical institution where he could get help. The strategy was clever, but it backfired. DeSalvo was sentenced to life in prison, exactly what he had wanted so badly to avoid.

Gains and Losses

Why did all the people who distrusted DeSalvo's story give up on finding the real killer? In many cases, they had no choice. Their complaints had gone unheard by their bosses. Their questions had been ignored. Their roles in the case had been eliminated or replaced.

Besides, there was a lot to lose if DeSalvo was revealed as the wrong guy. Fairly or unfairly, the Strangler Task Force and the various police departments would lose their hero status and once again become a laughingstock.

Reputations boosted by DeSalvo's confession would be broken if that confession proved false. In addition, a lot of money was on the line. A movie was being made about the Boston Strangler, just as DeSalvo had hoped, and several key players in the Strangler drama were paid significant sums of cash for their expertise or the use of their real names.

Detective Philip DiNatale was paid $4,000 to be a consultant on the film, which was quite a bit of money at the time. Later, he started his own private investigation firm. Edward Brooke, the attorney general who created the task force to hunt down

Name Change

In the film *The Boston Strangler*, the victims' names were changed to maintain their privacy. There were other major changes. One of the biggest revisions in the movie is the John Bottomly character. The movie portrays him as a tough, relentless man who races from one crime scene to another. In reality, he may never have visited the scene of a single crime.

the Strangler, was reportedly paid $20,000 for the use of his name in the movie. He also became a senator. John Bottomly, the recently resigned chief of the Strangler Task Force, sold the rights to his and his family's life story for $29,000. He was made the hero of the film.

DeSalvo and his family made some money off both the book and the movie, but nowhere near as much as DeSalvo assumed he would. Interestingly, Bottomly served as the attorney for DeSalvo's wife when she sold the rights to her and her children's names for $25,000.

The Strangler was not a phantom after all; his vanishing act was over. Soon, moviegoers would be able to see him in theaters across the country. But before they did, he found a way to vanish one more time. On February 24, 1967, the self-proclaimed Boston Strangler disappeared.

Not-So-Great Escape

At first, nobody was sure what had happened. An orderly had checked on DeSalvo that morning and swore he had been in his room sleeping. But he was gone. And two other inmates had vanished as well.

One of them—it is not clear which—had stolen a key from an orderly. All three had arranged the sheets on their beds so it looked like they were still sleeping, then hurried to an elevator and climbed down the shaft. They scaled one wall and then another, then drove off in a stolen car.

As far as the people of Massachusetts were concerned, the Boston Strangler was once again on the loose. One woman reportedly wielded a shotgun as she did housework. Another woman forbid her 12-year-old boy to leave the house for two days. The *Record American* offered a $5,000 reward for the Strangler, dead or alive. Bailey offered $10,000, but only if he was brought in alive.

DeSalvo made it only 40 miles (64 km) from Bridgewater. He broke into a cellar and stayed there for the night. The next afternoon, he walked into a store, called Bailey, and waited by the water cooler for the police to come.

By the time the cops showed up, 2,000 people had gathered around the store to get a look at the

Mob Violence

The crowd of people who gathered around cop cars after DeSalvo's escape included townspeople and reporters. Some were there to stare, but others were out for blood. "Kill him!" they shouted.[5] DeSalvo, never one to avoid the spotlight, gave some dramatic winks to the crowd before ducking into the squad car.

Boston Strangler. Once he was back in custody, DeSalvo claimed he had attempted the escape to show he was sick and needed to get help at a medical institution.

The Boston Strangler came out in 1968. It was a hit with moviegoers and critics. If the general public had had any lingering doubts about DeSalvo's identity, they did no longer. He had gone on trial as the Green Man but had been convicted—by the court of public opinion, anyway—as the Boston Strangler.

A crowd heckles DeSalvo, *lower left-hand corner in black,* as he is captured and returned to custody following his 1967 escape.

Chapter 10

The Strangler Today

Two decades later, Casey Sherman saw _The Boston Strangler_ for the first time. Sherman's mother, Diane Dodd, was Mary Sullivan's sister but had been reluctant to talk about her. Sherman knew his aunt was the Strangler's last victim, but he knew little else.

Finally, having stumbled upon the movie while clicking through channels, he mustered up the courage to ask his mother about his aunt. In a pained voice, Dodd shared her memories of her sister. Trying to console his mother, Sherman said, "At least they got the guy."[1]

To his surprise, his mother disagreed. As far as she was concerned, her sister's killer had never been caught. Curious, Sherman decided to research the issue further. The more research he did, the more he realized his mother was not alone; many other people—people who knew DeSalvo or had worked on his case—agreed that DeSalvo could not have been the Strangler. One of these people was Richard DeSalvo—DeSalvo's brother.

Mary Sullivan's sister Diane Dodd and nephew Casey Sherman pose with a picture of Mary.

The Brother Behind Bars

Once DeSalvo was put away for the rest of his life, most people who knew him did their best to forget him—but not Richard. He and his wife frequently visited DeSalvo in prison.

Oddly, Nassar—at one time a top Strangler suspect—was always present during these visits. Why did DeSalvo insist on including him during family time? Once, Richard remembers, DeSalvo asked him if he wanted to know who the *real* Strangler was. Then he pointed to the man sitting next to him—Nassar. Was DeSalvo kidding, or telling his brother the truth?

At another visit, DeSalvo looked uncharacteristically nervous. He said things were really tense at that time and that he was about to speak up about something. He did not clarify what he meant, but he did tell his brother not to come see him for a while. Then he hugged Richard, something he

Writing a Book?

There were rumors that DeSalvo was writing a manuscript about the real story behind the Strangler, but after his death it was never found. DeSalvo did write a poem about the Strangler while in prison. The last two lines are "People everywhere are still in doubt, Is the Strangler in prison, or roaming about?"[2]

rarely, if ever, did. This visit was the last time Richard saw his brother alive.

On November 26, 1973, DeSalvo's body was found in the prison infirmary. He had been stabbed repeatedly in the heart.

Silenced Confession

Some claim DeSalvo was killed in a fight over some bacon. Others say the fight had to do with drugs. DeSalvo had become a drug dealer, some say, and he had angered the wrong people.

Richard DeSalvo poses with a photo of his brother, whom he believes was innocent of the Boston stranglings despite Albert's confession.

But Dr. Robey has another theory. Dr. Robey had not spoken with DeSalvo in years, but the night before his death, DeSalvo called Robey and a reporter and asked them to visit. "He was going to tell us who the Boston Strangler really was," said Robey.[3]

Was DeSalvo killed to silence his confession? DeSalvo spent 54 hours giving a confession that many today consider bogus. But he may have never gotten the chance to give a real confession, one that would have finally revealed the identity of the Boston Strangler.

Whether or not DeSalvo was killed to keep him quiet, the method of his murder was particularly chilling. There was a reason DeSalvo had spent the night in the infirmary: it was the safest place in the prison. To get to DeSalvo, an inmate would have had to get through more than half a dozen locked doors. Guards were supposed to be stationed at several of these doors.

No one knows how the killer got in, or whether the guards provided keys

NO CONVICTIONS: Two men were charged with killing DeSalvo. Both trials ended in mistrials. No one was ever convicted in the case.

or opened the doors themselves. DeSalvo's murder remains as unsolved as the Boston Stranglings.

Back to the Present

By the 1990s, it had become Casey Sherman's mission to find his aunt's murderer. The case had been abandoned for decades. But Sherman had new technology at his disposal: DNA testing.

The first places Sherman went to get DNA samples were the Boston Police Department and the attorney general's office. He had seen a list of evidence from Sullivan's case file and was hoping to test some of it for DNA remains. Maybe there was a hair left on an object, or some blood or saliva.

But both the police department and the attorney general's office claimed the evidence was gone or had deteriorated too badly for testing. Sherman was skeptical. There were 245 items on the list of evidence. He did not believe that every single one was unusable.

After a series of meetings—both in offices and in courtrooms—Sherman finally accepted that he might never be given access to the evidence, and he began looking for other ways to find DNA samples. If he could not test the objects taken from Sullivan's apartment all those years ago, he would test the people themselves.

In October 2000, Sullivan's remains were unearthed. Sherman asked James Starrs to perform the exhumation. Starrs was famous for his expertise in forensic science. When Starrs and his team got to Sullivan's casket, they discovered the cover of the casket had caved in, allowing the casket itself to fill with water. At first, no one knew if the water damage would make it hard for Starrs to obtain samples. All Sherman could do was wait and hope.

On July 18, 2001, Richard DeSalvo let a physician take his blood and saliva for DNA testing. As Albert DeSalvo's brother, his DNA closely matched his sibling's. By comparing Richard's DNA to the DNA left at Sullivan's crime scene, one could determine whether there were any similarities.

Sherman and Richard announced they were willing to share the results of Richard's DNA testing with the current Boston attorney general if the attorney general shared his evidence with them. His response was succinct: no deal.

What the Dead Can Tell Us

On October 26, 2001, DeSalvo was exhumed. Unlike Sullivan's exhumation, which had been done publicly, DeSalvo's body was unearthed in secrecy. Only Starrs's team and a few others were present.

Sullivan's body is exhumed while Starrs, center with beard, looks on.

After getting the body into an SUV hearse, the team traveled to York College in Pennsylvania where a lab was waiting for them. The autopsy took place the next day. As with Sullivan's body, all that was left to do was wait for the results.

Finally, on December 6, 2001, more than three decades after DeSalvo announced he had killed

DNA from the Dead

Even after years of decay, a dead body can still reveal a lot through DNA testing. An example of this occurred in 1995. Starrs and his team dug up the body under outlaw Jesse James's tomb. For a long time there had been rumors that James had faked his own death; if that were true, the body Starrs dug up would not be James's. DNA testing proved these rumors were false. The man in the tomb was indeed James.

Sullivan, Starrs and his team held a press conference to announce whether DeSalvo had been telling the truth.

First, Michael Baden, a pathologist, went over some of the problems with DeSalvo's confession. Professor Bruce Goldberger, a toxicologist, explained that there were no drugs or alcohol in Mary Sullivan's body at the time she was killed. Professor David Foran, who has a background in DNA profiling, said two different foreign substances had indeed been found on Sullivan's body. However, neither came from DeSalvo. It could now be stated with complete confidence that DeSalvo was not Sullivan's killer.

Back to the Drawing Board

Who was the Boston Strangler? Likely, it was more than one man. Possibly many more. Of the 11 stranglings, many believe only the first five look similar enough to have been carried out by one man. Even then, it is possible some were copycat murderers. There are several prime suspects for these crimes, all of whom appear to have the means and the motive to commit such atrocities.

The only aspect the next six killings had in common was that all but one of the victims were young. Other than that, their murders were drastically different.

Patricia Bissette was tucked into bed; Mary Sullivan was left sitting on top of the bed. Jane Sullivan was left facedown in a tub; Ida Irga was left propped up on a chair. The list of differences goes on and on. The evidence is inconclusive. Who killed these women? Unless the cases are reopened, only the killer or killers will know for sure.

Tools and Clues

autopsy— Criminal pathologists perform a thorough investigation of a dead body to determine how, why, when and where a crime was committed. As modern forensic technology improves, pathologists are able to find more clues that were once undetectable. After Mary Sullivan's body was exhumed, two different DNA samples were discovered on her body.

DNA testing— By analyzing the skin, hair, or fluid on a body, forensic scientists can help determine the innocence or guilt of a criminal suspect. Albert DeSalvo's DNA was not found on Mary Sullivan's body.

exhumation— This involves digging up dead bodies to subject them to further analysis. Mary Sullivan's and Albert DeSalvo's bodies were exhumed.

fingerprinting– One way investigators narrow down suspects is to analyze fingerprints left at the crime scene. A handprint was found on a television in Beverly Samans's apartment, but experts determined it did not belong to Albert DeSalvo.

lie detector– This machine records an increase in heart rate or blood pressure. Typically, such an increase suggests a person is lying. Jules Rothman failed a lie detector test after Patricia Bissette's murder.

police sketch– An artist attempts to draw a picture of a suspect based on a witness's description. An investigator recognized Albert DeSalvo when looking at a sketch of the Green Man. On the other hand, no sketches of the man (or men) who likely committed the Boston stranglings looked anything like DeSalvo.

toxicology screen– This test analyzes blood or urine samples to determine whether drugs or alcohol were consumed before a crime took place. Mary Sullivan's test for toxins was clean.

Timeline

1961   Several sexual assaults take place in Cambridge, Massachusetts, by a man—soon dubbed the Measuring Man—posing as a representative of Black and White Modeling Agency.

1962   On June 14, Anna Slesers becomes the first reported Boston Strangler victim.

1962   Nina Nichols and Helen Blake are found dead on June 30.

1962   Ida Irga is found dead on August 19.

1962   Jane Sullivan is found dead on August 20.

1962.   Sophie Clark is
        murdered on
        December 5.

1962.   On December 31,
        Patricia Bissette
        is murdered. Jules
        Rothman becomes
        a suspect in her
        murder and the
        Strangler murders.

1963   On February 18, Erika Wilsing fights off
        an attacker. She is thought to be the only
        survivor of the Boston Strangler.

1963   A woman is attacked and nearly strangled
        on April 9. Arthur Barrows becomes another
        suspect in the Strangler case.

1963   On May 5, Beverly Samans is murdered.
        Daniel Pennacchio takes credit for the
        murder.

1963   Evelyn Corbin is murdered on September 8.
        Robert Cambell becomes a suspect.

Timeline

<u>1963</u>	Joann Graff is found dead on November 23.
<u>1964</u>	Mary Sullivan's dead body is found on January 4.

<u>1964</u>	Peter Burton is arrested on January 22. He becomes a strangler suspect.
<u>1964</u>	On September 29, a man later identified as George Nassar shoots a man at a gas station. Nassar becomes a suspect in the Strangler cases.
<u>1964</u>	On October 27, Suzanne Macht is sexually assaulted by the Green Man.

1965 From August to September, Albert DeSalvo describes to officials how he killed the 11 Strangler victims. There are holes in his confession.

1973 DeSalvo is killed in prison.

2000 Mary Sullivan's remains are exhumed.

2001 DeSalvo's body is exhumed by forensic scientists.

2001 Forensic scientists announce that two foreign substances were found on Sullivan's body. Neither of them came from DeSalvo.

Glossary

autopsy . . . . An examination of a body to determine the cause of death.

confession . . . . An admission of committing a crime.

exhume . . . . To dig up a body from its grave.

forensic. . . . . Using science to solve crimes.

housecoat . . . . An informal, lightweight robe worn by women around the house.

incarcerate . . . . To imprison.

interrogate .... To question a suspect of a crime.

parole .... A release of a prisoner with certain
conditions or limitations.

photographic
memory .... The ability to recall information in great
detail.

polygraph .... A machine used to detect when a person is
lying.

profile .... A description of likely characteristics of
a criminal based on clues found at crime
scenes.

serial killer ...... A person who has committed more than one
murder on separate occasions. Generally
the series of murders have shared
characteristics.

sexual assault ..... A physical attack involving touching
a person's body in a sexual way without
consent.

toxicologist .... A specialist who studies poisons.

Additional Resources

Selected Bibliography

Bardsley, Marilyn. "The Boston Strangler." *TruTV Crime Library*. Turner Entertainment, 2011. Web. 1 Nov. 2011.

Kelly, Susan. *The Boston Stranglers*. New York: Kessington, 1995. Print.

Rogers, Alan. *The Boston Strangler*. Beverly, MA: Commonwealth, 2006. Print.

Sherman, Casey. *Search for the Strangler: My Hunt for Boston's Most Notorious Killer*. New York: Warner, 2003. Print.

Further Readings

DK Editors. *Forensic Science*. New York: DK, 2008. Print.

Hamilton, Sue L. *Forensic Artist: Solving the Case with a Face*. Edina, MN: ABDO, 2008. Print.

Web Links

To learn more about the Boston Strangler, visit ABDO Publishing Company online at **www.abdopublishing.com**. Web sites about the Boston Strangler are featured on our Book Links page. These links are routinely monitored and updated to provide the most current information available.

Places to Visit

Ghosts and Gravestones Frightseeing Tour
Corner of Atlantic Avenue and State Street, Boston, MA 02110
617-269-3626
http://www.ghostsandgravestones.com/boston
On this tour, you can explore the streets once stalked by the Boston Strangler.

National Museum of Crime & Punishment
575 Seventh Street NW Washington, DC 20004
202-621-5550
http://www.crimemuseum.org
At this museum, you can discover the history of crime and punishment in the United States.

Source Notes

Chapter 1. Case Closed?

1. Robert J. Anglin. "DeSalvo is 'Boston Strangler': Defense Says He Killed 13." *Boston Globe* 13 Jan. 1967. Print.

2. Alan Rogers. *The Boston Strangler.* Beverly, MA: Commonwealth, 2006. Print. 3.

3. Susan Kelly. *The Boston Stranglers.* New York: Kessington, 1995. Print. 418–419.

Chapter 2. A Tense Town

1. "Another Silk Stocking Murder; Lynn Nurse, 65, Strangled Same Day as Brighton Woman, 68." *Boston Globe* 3 July 1962. Print.

2. "Police Hunt Mad Triple Killer; Warn Women Living Alone: Keep Door Locked." *Boston Globe* 4 July 1962. Print.

3. Susan Kelly. *The Boston Stranglers.* New York: Kessington, 1995. Print. 30.

4. Irene Michaleck, Jack Wharton, and Bill Duncliffe. "Phantom Strangler Strikes Again, Back Bay Secretary 8th Victim." *Record American* 1 Jan. 1963. Print.

5. Susan Kelly. *The Boston Stranglers.* New York: Kessington, 1995. Print. 493.

6. Gerold Frank. *The Boston Strangler.* New York: New American Library, 1966. Print. 15.

7. Ibid. 40.

8. Marilyn Bardsley. "The Boston Strangler." *TruTV Crime Library.* Turner Entertainment, 2011. Web. 17 Sept. 2011.

9. Ibid.

10. Gerold Frank. *The Boston Strangler.* New York: New American Library, 1966. Print. 168.

11. Ibid.

12. Susan Kelly. *The Boston Stranglers.* New York: Kessington, 1995. Print. 48–50.

13. Gerold Frank. *The Boston Strangler.* New York: New American Library, 1966. Print. 89.

Chapter 3. <u>The Measuring Man</u>

1. Susan Kelly. *The Boston Stranglers*. New York: Kessington, 1995. Print. 249.

2. Casey Sherman. *Search for the Strangler: My Hunt for Boston's Most Notorious Killer*. New York: Warner, 2003. Print. 48.

3. Ibid. 54.

4. Susan Kelly. *The Boston Stranglers*. New York: Kessington, 1995. Print. 81.

5. Casey Sherman. *Search for the Strangler: My Hunt for Boston's Most Notorious Killer*. New York: Warner, 2003. Print. 93.

Chapter 4. <u>Suspect under Scrutiny</u>

1. Susan Kelly. *The Boston Stranglers*. New York: Kessington, 1995. Print. 72–74.

2. Alan Rogers. *The Boston Strangler*. Beverly, MA: Commonwealth, 2006. Print. 38.

3. Susan Kelly. *The Boston Stranglers*. New York: Kessington, 1995. Print. 229.

4. Casey Sherman. *Search for the Strangler: My Hunt for Boston's Most Notorious Killer*. New York: Warner, 2003. Print. 90.

Chapter 5. No Positive IDs

1. Susan Kelly. *The Boston Stranglers*. New York: Kessington, 1995. Print. 235.
2. Ibid. 237.
3. Ibid. 236.
4. Ibid. 235–237.

Chapter 6. DeSalvo's Confession

1. Susan Kelly. *The Boston Stranglers*. New York: Kessington, 1995. Print. 252.
2. Casey Sherman. *Search for the Strangler: My Hunt for Boston's Most Notorious Killer*. New York: Warner, 2003. Print. 81.
3. Susan Kelly. *The Boston Stranglers*. New York: Kessington, 1995. Print. 277.
4. Ibid. 239.

Chapter 7. The Real Boston Strangler

1. Susan Kelly. *The Boston Stranglers*. New York: Kessington, 1995. Print. 316, 320.

Chapter 8. More Suspects

1. Susan Kelly. *The Boston Stranglers*. New York: Kessington, 1995. Print. 345.
2. Casey Sherman. *Search for the Strangler: My Hunt for Boston's Most Notorious Killer*. New York: Warner, 2003. Print. 33.

Chapter 9. <u>A Madman's Motives</u>

1. Casey Sherman. *Search for the Strangler: My Hunt for Boston's Most Notorious Killer.* New York: Warner, 2003. Print. 64.

2. Susan Kelly. *The Boston Stranglers.* New York: Kessington, 1995. Print. 124.

3. Ibid. 74.

4. Ibid. 136.

5. Casey Sherman. *Search for the Strangler: My Hunt for Boston's Most Notorious Killer.* New York: Warner, 2003. Print. 94–95.

Chapter 10. <u>The Strangler Today</u>

1. Casey Sherman. *Search for the Strangler: My Hunt for Boston's Most Notorious Killer.* New York: Warner, 2003. Print. 90.

2. Ibid. 103.

3. Marilyn Bardsley. "The Boston Strangler." *TruTV Crime Library.* Turner Entertainment, 2011. Web. 17 Sept. 2011.

Index

About the Author

Paul Hoblin received his MFA in Creative Writing from the University of Minnesota.

About the Content Consultant

Jim Collins began his investigative career with the Federal Drug Enforcement Administration in 1978 and founded East Coast Investigative Services in 1988. He helped Casey Sherman in his search for the real Boston Strangler.

Photo Credits